Praise for *savir*

"If you point me in the
  I'd run inside and scre:

"For if God saves her,
  she will save us.

"She is not writing for the sake of poetry,
  But for the sake of our souls."
                    —Jasmine Mans, author of *Black Girl, Call Home*

"Roya Marsh has offered a collection of work for those who are
ready to feel something, to remember something, to imagine
something. *savings time* invites us, above all, to be honest with
ourselves about the world we live in—Marsh gives us the lan-
guage to do so."
                    —Rachel Cargle, author of *A Renaissance of Our Own*

"Scientists have reported that time is literally speeding up. How-
ever, Roya Marsh's new work reminds us that it is Black, queer
artists who bend time, who sculpt it with language and truth.
These poems ask us to reclaim our time, to tenderly coax the
future from the hands of so much oppression. This work re-
minds us that it is indeed us who will save time."
                    —Sonya Renee Taylor, author of *The Body Is Not an Apology*

"In a world of too much curation that desperately clings to perfor-
mative patterns and homogeneous hashtags, Roya Marsh's *sav-
ings time* is your beloved, your breaking heart, your own mirror
gently beckoning you out of every useless facade of restraint
or good behavior and back into the light of all that still lingers.

Marsh's poems remind us what poems can do: uncover, unshame, and unbury." —Candice Iloh, author of *Salt the Water*

"In *savings time*, Roya Marsh sharpens her words like a razor, cutting through the layers of identity, trauma, and defiance with a voice that is as relentless as it is tender. These poems are not just read but felt, each one a visceral reminder of the ongoing struggle to exist fully in a world that too often attempts to erase you. Marsh's poetry collection is a fierce, unapologetic, and bluesy anthem for anyone who's ever been told they're too much or not enough."

—Frederick Joseph, bestselling author of *We Alive, Beloved*

"I started reading Roya Marsh's words and after the first few pages had to put the book down. It was too powerful! As I continued, the pacing made me feel like I was on the A train between 59th and 125th—that long stretch of speed with no stops in between, where I get lost in my thoughts gazing at fellow passengers, while the car shakes my body into a jiggle. *That* is how *savings time* made me feel. Roya Marsh's writing is unapologetically from the block without the code switch, expressed for our people to provoke, inspire, and uplift. If only the world could be this intelligent and empathetic." —Bobbito García, a.k.a. Kool Bob Love

"*savings time* is a book you gift to your favorite cousin, the one who is right on the verge of a breakthrough but just can't get the words out of their mouth. Because it is not just a book of poems. It is a promise. Roya Marsh writes like she really believes we can be free. I believe her."

—EbonyJanice Moore, author of *All the Black Girls Are Activists*

Roya Marsh

savings time

Roya Marsh is a native of the Bronx, New York, and a nationally recognized poet, performer, educator, and activist. She is the author of the poetry collection *dayliGht*, which was a finalist for the 2021 Lambda Literary Award for Lesbian Poetry. Marsh works feverishly toward Queer liberation and the dismantling of white supremacy. She is the cofounder of the position of Bronx Poet Laureate, a PEN America Emerging Voices mentor, a member of the Lambda Literary faculty, and the recipient of the Lotos Foundation Prize for poetry.

Marsh is a former poet in residence at Urban Word NYC, and her work has been featured by NBC, BET, Button Poetry, Def Jam's All Def Digital, the Academy of American Poets, BAM, Carnegie Hall, the Kennedy Center, the Apollo Theater, and Lexus Verses and Flow. She has been published in *Poetry, The Village Voice, Nylon, HuffPost, The Root, On One with Angela Rye*, and in the collection *The BreakBeat Poets Vol. 2: Black Girl Magic*.

Also by Roya Marsh

dayliGht: poems

savings time

savings time

Poems

Roya Marsh

MCD Farrar, Straus and Giroux • New York

MCD
Farrar, Straus and Giroux
120 Broadway, New York 10271

Library of Congress Cataloging-in-Publication Data
Names: Marsh, Roya, 1988– author.
Title: savings time : poems / Roya Marsh.
Description: First edition. | New York : MCD / Farrar, Straus and Giroux, 2025.
Identifiers: LCCN 2024034087 | ISBN 9780374615796 (paperback)
Subjects: LCGFT: Poetry.
Classification: LCC PS3613.A76987 S28 2025 | DDC 811/.6—dc23/eng/20240724
LC record available at https://lccn.loc.gov/2024034087

Designed by Gretchen Achilles

Our books may be purchased in bulk for promotional, educational,
or business use. Please contact your local bookseller or the Macmillan
Corporate and Premium Sales Department at 1-800-221-7945,
extension 5442, or by email at MacmillanSpecialMarkets@macmillan.com.

www.mcdbooks.com • www.fsgbooks.com
Follow us on social media at @mcdbooks and @fsgbooks

10   9   8   7   6   5   4   3   2   1

For Tonya Ingram and everyone who deserved more time

There is no time for despair, no place for self-pity, no need for silence, no room for fear. We speak, we write, we do language. That is how civilizations heal.

—Toni Morrison,
"No Place for Self-Pity, No Room for Fear,"
The Nation, March 2015

There is never a time in the future in which we will work out our salvation. The challenge is in the moment; the time is always now.

—James Baldwin, *Nobody Knows My Name*

Contents

A Note from the Author

They never wanted us to read. That should tell you all you need to know about why I continue to write. I was born loud with my mouth wide open. My affinity for spoken word came as no surprise to me, but my journey into publishing is a story for the ages. *dayliGht*, my first book, was the most daring thing I had ever written and it changed my life forever. It offered readers a glimpse into my evolution from "tomboy" to Butch woman and ushered me closer to my own liberation. This book, *savings time*, is not a follow-up; it is a time capsule. It is a deep imprint on the fabric of society. It is a pursuit. I have expanded in my purpose and cite self-love and literacy as great emancipators. "I'm no better if I only save myself." I am after our collective Black liberation and know that our revolution needs all of us. I'm bringing with me as many people as I can.

There are days when I am weary to my soul. But people everywhere are dying to live free and that ancestral vigor is in me. I know I have to live. I vow to be myself. Authentically. Audaciously. In your face. Not in spite of anyone. Simply because it is my right. That alone is enough for someone to want me dead.

Every page you read is going to require you to be as honest with yourself as possible. These poems want you to ask questions and to think critically about how you engage with the world around you. These poems are going to encourage you to find joy in the ordinary. These poems are a love letter to my friends. A love letter to hip-hop. A love letter to my Blackness. A love letter to *my* Queerness. A love letter to the culture. These poems want you to know your power.

They are banning books and bodies; it is only a matter of time before they come for our last breath.

What are you waiting for?

savings time

What are the rights to your existence?

I have the right to remain loud as fuck.
Anything you say can and will be used in a poem, a lecture, or
    a screenshot.
I have the right to talk my shit before I let you finish.
I have the right to bring my goons with me wherever I go.
If I'm touching greatness, I plan to share it.
If I cannot afford to burn a bridge, reconciliation is a must.
If I decide to give a second chance and you let me down,
I have the right to liberate myself at any time.

Visions

I have seen more caskets lowered beneath grounds than I have seen caps and gowns. I have heard the heartbeats of babies aborted, had visions of lives they could've been afforded. I have known more fatherless sons than churches know nuns. And priests . . . preying, on the meek. Laying on the weak. Whisper while they sneak, make sure the pew doesn't creak. I have seen the innocent made guilty. The clean appear filthy. The filthy appear clean. Corruption is a helluva drug. I mean, I've seen backs turned to the truth to preserve a lie. I've seen backs facing the roof as brothers lose lives. I've seen families cry, as their children have died without a reason why.

I have seen the "news" give out information that is old and watched all you believe everything you are told. But you care more that Kanye and Kim named their baby Saint, Psalm, or after the North Pole. Or what to fear more, UFOs or GMOs, when there's not much of a difference. We're already clones. Already drones. Our marrow becomes narrow in our feeble bones. Our brains attached to these mobile phones. The whole state of NY is a mobile home. You can't stay still in a city that never sleeps . . . always on the creep . . . wear your mask but the poison still seeps. The weepers still weep. The reaper still reaps . . . you stopped listening yet? 'Cause I ain't even went that deep.

I have seen the nameless beg for names, doing anything for fame. The homeless beg for change, watch you say "I cannot spare" as you pull off in your Range. These days they're snatching people, no more use in snatching chains. Crooks and cops are not so different, they just do as they've been trained. The innocent are framed so status quos may be maintained. Reps are being stained, lives are being slain, and the verdict is not guilty when the cops get arraigned. So much for global warming, I think the earth's about to boil. I have seen what it is like to be caught in the law's toil. You can shoot down teenage Black boys and watch their dreams be foiled. But you cannot stand your ground if your skin resembles soil.

I have seen equality appear only as a mirage. The media throws shade as the eager public is barraged. I have seen us being set back by 69 & a beef with Ms. Minaj. Right back into minstrelsy it seems we've gladly delved. I've seen the support of the exploiters as the makeup leaves the shelves. They ain't gotta dress in Blackface no more when we do that by ourselves. I have seen a Black man in the White House . . . I thought we proved a point. Then they elected *you know who* & that proved to disappoint.

They will do what they can to assure we remain pawns. I have seen more white house puppies instead of what's really going on. They want to worry us about the world while they've been gassing us for years. Making us *"think they gave us us free"* when our freedom is their biggest fear.

These days I hang my head a lot. I'm losing hope. 'Cause this is greater than a scandal between President Fitz and Olivia Pope. But I can only count on one hand the friends I have that vote. Sometimes I think this shit is a joke. I've seen that death has no preference when it wants to take us down. It really doesn't matter if our skin is white or brown. I've seen suicide seem appealing when I was emotionally gagged and bound. I've seen drugs taking souls, leaving bodies to be found. If you OD when no one is listening does your dead body make a sound?

There's a war going on right here in your hometown. You'll never see it if you don't look around.

The truth

my only fear is fear
and fear ain't real
when i say i'm that deal
it's already signed and sealed
woman's heart of steel
gentlemen's sex appeal
intelligence of an elephant
forever keeping it real
they banning books and bodies
while we steady tryna heal
only matter of time 'fore
our breath they tryna steal

my dreams got realer
when my mouth got bigger.
they say, *how you know you dope?*
You act like you that nigga!
i say i thought life was mine,
God was like, *how you figure?*
took a look at my reflection
saw a savior in the glimpser.
i was the one in front of the gun
& the one behind the trigger.
Self-love and depression
is one hell of a mixture.

coulda ended it all
in the blink of a finger.
Silence is deafening
shots don't whisper.
who am i to make my death come quicker?
record this shit, click that picture.
come get this good news.
call me scripture.

a graduate that don't ask for shit
on road, 'bout to explode, still no management
i'm into saving time, no bullshit kinda anarchist
i'm my own daddy, i make my own sugar, *they* mad at this

but i'ma write the next book,
they gon' publish these hot poems
we gon' stack this paper and build us some Black homes
with colorful gardens, green pastures with Black gnomes
me and my queen so in love, we gon' make us some Black
    clones
keep the wealth in the fam, we gon' give out some Black loans
no more killin' our mans, we got us some backbones
i mean every word i say, hope you catch my exact tone.

Admissions of guilt

i play with the dead
or almost
my favorite songs say the word nigga
or bitch
my favorite poems are suicidal
or homicidal
or genocidal
there's something about pain that makes me feel good
or real
I don't quite know how to feel happy
or whole
I'm told you're not to feel it, but to be it
i am broken
i love to see others like me
so i break them
i am guilty of not fixing the things i have broken
starting with myself
i just become a newer version
of the same broken
i've always been
i hold the me now accountable
for the me i was then
it gets me nowhere
they hold the me now accountable
for the me i was then

it gets us nowhere
i am guilty of breaking things
and people
like me
they are guilty of staying broken

Sometimes what doesn't kill me makes me wish i were dead

surviving is a slow decay
corrupted healing of the mind that refuses to forget how i
    was almost a memory
a few more inches to the left and that would have been all she
    wrote
a day late and the cure'd be useless
one false move and i am
never again
      the night after the pills
a gulp of swallows
on a power line
      sing me into Wednesday
the sun heckles me through a hospital window &
i'm s'posta rejoice
while death takes a ticket
impatiently waits for the red light above a window to call me
home—another place i'd rather not

Today   my pronouns are
Black and Alive

This one

for the bad bitches/that rarely get called on/the big
foreheads/big heads/lil heads/cock-eyed/eyeglasses/
unibrow/gaptooth smiles/stubborn hairs above the lip/
below the lip/extra peach fuzz/with the saggy titties/lil extra
around the middle/round the side/big back/lotta extra all
ova/semi tight jeans/belly hangin' ova/lil miss nuffin'/
flat booty/ittybittytittycommittee/bag of bones/
nice toes/hammer toes/big feet/lil ones/daddy issues/
mommy issues/issue issues

you are worthy right now
go where there is love
your flowers are waiting

Remember that time

the check was late
the rent was due
traction alopecia snatchin'
whatever edges the IRS left
you arguing with love
about brownies and kissin'
so much that kissin' seem like work
and we ain't s'posed to be workin'
we s'posed to have distance
while dyin' to be social with anyone,
but each other
you found yourself missin' the train
you're too anxious to take
just to avoid that feeling
the walls milking the doubt from you
and your first book dropped
but no one picked it up 'cause they were all home
too worried or sick or jobless or preoccupied
with being unoccupied
too busy to read your book about you
and your view on the world no one can even get to
you thought you knew
all you needed to know,
when the days blended together
and sun never seemed to rise,

the crisp of night is all you had
to remind yourself of mo(u)rning
that like you
it even existed
sometimes needing a reminder
minor & clumsy like condensation
on a backseat window
you never meant to breathe
on, as foolish as your reflection
scribbled by a fingertip,
where there is always a smile, even if you can't
you paint one on
when your will to live is suspended in air
and only gathers to cackle you stupid
for trying, asking:
how you're still here
you trick yourself into living
daily, constantly keeping your insides
inside is an inside job,
you ask yourself these questions
who is better because of you?
what will come of what you leave behind?
do you
remember that time
you survived?

Admissions of guilt, too

there are all kinds of guilt
sometimes it manifests as a broken promise
another fist through plaster
shattered teeth, shattered egos
thought i had been honest with myself
with the world
i was dancing around the fire
taunting the flames
accepted this pattern of misuse and
became its fuel

if i were really admitting guilt
i would have said, *i think i needed it*
i would have said, *hit me, again*
another wound, another chapter in my villain origin story
i would have said the panic felt like home
but that's just not something you can say
when they ask   *why didn't you just leave?*
if i were really admitting guilt
i would have said i still think i deserve to die
i still wouldn't have said your name
even though i still count the syllables

guilt is a life partner
a driving force

comes spilling out of me
all my unmentionables trailing behind
like a swerving U-Haul in rush hour traffic
guilt is the reason for my silence and my revolution

if i were really admitting guilt
i would have said, *I am sorry*
i forgive you
to myself

we changed the way we thought about birthdays
Like, instead of splurging on some milestone party
You get gifts for all of your closest homies and go to their
    houses to drop them off
and give a 2 minute speech about how dope they are
What if we don't do cake?
What if we do iced matcha with oatmilk (for my stomach)
What if we took a drive to the middle of nowhere and shouted
    at the top of our lungs for as long as our throats would let
    us
What if we don't sing? anything! Nope. Not even *that one*
What if we smoked ourselves stiff and binged *Atlanta* on FX
What if we . . . shit, I might do that rn
What if we forego decorations and just like . . . clean this
    place
What if we didn't answer every happy birthday heart-eyes,
    winky, thumbs-up, confetti text with generic iMessage
    balloons
What if folks didn't race to FaceTime the birthday person at
    midnight
What if the day just went how you needed it to go
What if we get life insurance for all our friends, go casket
    shopping, pick a plot, pick an urn, an ocean to scatter
    what's left of ourselves
Have a seat on the shore and cry for the fuck of it, crack a

brew & have a drunk nap in the sand 'til the rain drives us
home
What if while we're living we learned to rest
in peace

Having a panic attack in the back seat of an Uber

fucking sucks. It's like being asked to hold a baby that just doesn't like your vibe. You know that blank stare babies give you that remind you to keep your day job. Yeah, he's doing that in the mirror between random anecdotes about traffic and NYC landscape. Yep, while the sweat is trickling down from your forehead to your tits & he just keeps doing this awkward half smile because you're laughing & crying & gasping for air all at once and the last time he saw this was when his wife had their 3rd child & no, it's not true what they say, it doesn't get easier after the first one. And you know this, because he's telling you, right now. As you can't help but grip the leather door handle wishing desperately to rip the whole thing off its hinges & fly it down the highway to safety like a magic carpet. You're trying to keep still, but it feels like a million things are crawling on the outside of you and the inside of you is up in flames. He rolls the windows down with your consent, given thru sobs, and the wind smacks the shit out of your flushed face, covered in chalk-like outlines from streams of indistinguishable sweat and tears. There are only two of you in this car until Big Freedia busts through the speaker reminding you to release your anger. You will want to. You'll speak. You have a simple request, but it is mutually impactful. His eyes wide as if to swallow all the tension. Your voice, slicing into the awkward, Would it be okay, if I screamed? He yells, YES! As if you've offered him millions & free healthcare and you'll feel a lil bit better about screaming, so you do. Ahhhhhh. And so does he. Ahhhh. You both take turns. Now, the whole East Side knows the sound of your voice. And the car is full of your breaths and your diaphragms are exhausted.

The energy is just calm enough for him to ask, what's going on?! And all you can say is, Everything is so expensive these days. Inflation is wild right now, he says . . . and you cut him off. When you say, *you can't afford things*, you mean, *you don't have enough time*. Every morning you wake up remembering you'll have one less day with your mother. And every time she calls to vent, which is really dumping, you think the laundry list of traumas she has survived is coming back to call her home. You think her mind is inching toward its final destination and you want to suggest she talk to someone, but she'll say she is talking to YOU! You want to put time in a savings account & only withdraw when you're ready to make your big purchase. You want your mother to live forever. And your mind cannot compute any equation that results in a world without her. I can't afford to miss a phone call. Or a birthday. Or a chance to hear her voice telling me the same story again and again. Concern blankets his face. His half smile is a straight line and once again you are sobbing.

Everyone is here to do a job, he says.

The car comes to a tender halt & he gently taps the horn.

Miss. We're here.

You look up & indeed, you are. Here.

How do we know who God is actually speaking to?
Is He speaking to racists?
Or the shop owner that follows Black customers around?
The father and son who pile into the pickup to hunt for a
  neighborhood jogger?
Is He speaking to the pastor
who buys luxury homes and cars while the congregation
  tithes for mercy?
Or to the platform preacher
condemning the Queer-less-than-woman, on her way to work,
to hell?
Or the father threatening to disown his firstborn?
Is He speaking to the mother
who straps her toddlers in a van and plows it into a body of
  water?
Is He speaking to the bombers before they strap destruction
  to their chests?
Or the officer before he pulls the trigger?
Is He speaking to the drunk driver doing 100 mph on a busy
  Texas freeway?
Or the silent whispers from the barrel of a gun
into the ear of a person at the end of their rope?
Is He speaking to the poor, the houseless, the loveless?
Does He say, "Stay that way! You can handle this battle! Don't
  give up!"

Is He speaking to his toughest soldiers
on their deathbeds?
Does He simply say, "You hadda good run, my child!" and
    close the curtains?
Is His voice deep? Is it loud? Does He know what that book
    says about Him? About me?
Does He believe it?
Does He evolve?
Is He passionate about anything other than His own will?
Is He speaking to anyone
Who will listen?
Is He even speaking?

Scorpion Unit: elegy for Tyre Nichols

on a fifty-degree night in January
the Mississippi River sings the blues.
the leaves whip to wind's tempo,
the moon is the only light
not controlled by the city.
all diurnal creatures retreat to shelter
and scorpions ascend from the mouths of burrows—
hungry. In search of prey.

A nearby siren warns Beware of Scorpions
Their behavior makes them one of the most feared
    organisms in the animal kingdom.
In any given neighborhood, you can find homes plagued
by them, while adjoining neighbors have never seen one.
Scorpions are solitary hunters, but they won't venture far
    from larger groups.
They move in units. This makes it easier to be predator.

It's rare for a scorpion sighting to be a one-time, random event.
There is always history.
Some sign of their presence.
Some fear of their return.

One time, trapped in a scorpion's cuffs,
I saw my life flash before its pincers.

wondered what a scorpion's threshold for fear is
before envenomation.
wondered what it thinks before it stings.
wondered who would fill my vacant burrow,
who would hold my mother,
who would tell my children I tried—
to make it home.

living dead

the first time
i stared down the barrel of an officer's gun.
i watched officer ██████ run his fingers up the thigh of my
   first love.

on a ten-minute drive
back to campus
we got pulled over
for *changing lanes*
with delayed indication.

after extensively viewing my license
officer ██████
proceeds to call me *sir*
"do you know why i pulled you over, sir"
"can i see your hands, sir"
"get out of the car, sir"
"you bull daggers like to be called sir, right?"

i am a first-generation Black Lesbian American.
they've been trying to deport my kind
to depression, to hatred, to hell.
each a place i've already dwelled.

i wanted to say *relax, babe*
everything will be fine
i'm not certain which one of us needed more assurance.

"get back in the car, sir
ma'am, could you step out please?
have you been drinking?"

"no, officer.
we just want to make it home, officer."

"yours or mine," he says

that year
sexual assault
was the second most common
form of misconduct reported
618 officers
with complaints
involving forcible
nonconsensual
sexual activity.

my palms
cemented
to the dash
staring through the rearview
i watched her quiver.

black streams
of eyeliner
rushing
down her face

that year,
the estimated amount
spent on misconduct-related
judgments and settlements
was over 346 million dollars

she surrendered her dignity
to his hands
so i could avoid
a $125 ticket.

this is the second time i regret exercising my right to remain
    silent.
there is no triumph in a tied tongue.

this is the first time i realize my weakness,
how is a woman
to protect herself
from a predator
with a badge,
a gun,
and a taste for
a woman's fear?

how likely are we to stand up for something
when the consequence
is time
in a cage or box
not much larger than the one we are
already trapped in?
her body
more than a sacrifice
on that night.
we chose a silent death,
sometimes suicide is a weaponless crime.

there is a graveyard
full of the words
i meant to say
when i settled for
i am sorry

for the rest of the way, i prayed
the radio could resurrect our night

that night,
i cried
in her sleep
mourned the people
we were
hours before
from the church pew in my sternum.

learned,
there are worse things
than watching someone die.
like lying
that close to her
decaying body
barely breathing

Blk Girl Puns

Knock, knock . . .
Who's there?
Black lives matter too
Black lives matter to who?
shrugs

New joke!
What do you call that useless skin around the vagina?
Nothing, if it's a Black woman.

Okay, okay . . . how 'bout this,
a father and daughter
walk into a bar—
no, each other's lives—
no, a park.
(I always get that part confused!)
A father & daughter
walk into a park
in <u>Brownsville</u>
to have beers
and/or sex
five teens approach
with or without a gun
father run
hahaha

Okay, okay. New joke
A father walks into a deli,
say, *lemme use your phone*
cashier don't say "*why?*"
don't say "*you ok?*"
he say "*no.*
you drunk.
you sway."
father run . . .
pass cop
in trouble
don't stop,
double back—
boys run,
<u>girl raped</u>.
News say more about playground & boy
than young woman treated as toy.
News say "alleged."
Her body say **full-fledged**.

*ain't that shit funny?
not funny *haha,*
more like, ain't it funny how
no one say assailants cry *consent*
when they inhabit a body; no rent.
They say Black girl
big lip

body thick
need dick.
Say, you wore that
Say, you did this
Say, it ain't rape even with a rape kit
Say, more about the cop you bit
Say, a park is no place to drink
Say, a bench is no place to fuck
Say, this just a Black girl's luck
Say, victim *cry* rape
Say, why ain't you escape?
Say, a drunken *yes*
means you wanted this–
to watch your obituary be headline
& you ain't even buried.
what?
they forgot to invite you
to your own homegoing?
this was your train, honey.
don't you know?
when 6 bodies
take hold of 1 body
they are pallbearers
to a [casket]
& your last rites on a
cellphone video.
a eulogy of drunken giggles.

nobody told you a Black girl's body is a punchline.
the funniest joke.
fit to be ran into the ground.

rimshot

i flipped a table once.

cups, plates, scattered
spaghetti massacre on laps.
all the restaurant alert
& this ga'damn TV
sayin' WE lost!

white girls vanish
the whole world grit they teeth,
but a Black girl's disappearance
warrants citywide curfews;
a second silencing
60 Black girls ghost
in the nation's capital
& my phone never rang about it!

64,000 in the world
and the Swifties ain't sanging 'bout it.
whole world a stop motion.
freeze frame.
stand still.

just that final gust of wind
that kills the candle.
*shiiiiit, WE already dead.

ain't no "epidemic"
of people being snatched.
it's a rite of passage.
every gentrified brick is
another brown future
collapsed into rubble!

no one told the Black girl
"see you later" was a prayer
begging us survive our own erasure.

they finna celebrate our absence
with silence. no sense
in giving white media the right to speak
for us

ain't no siren
news segment
no forest fire
or biblical flood
coming to make us anew

if nothing has tried to kill you
you have failed
bullet be to Black body
like our body be nothing at all
ain't no video of our maim & murder
cameras couldn't capture our kidnapping

our mama's tucking in a phantom
at night
an invisible vigil
a memorial
for the girl
the world has already forgotten

we gotta be our own
saviors
I'm fighting for you
got my eyes & ears peeled
knuckles bare & bloody
hoarse
you ain't gonna never be alone
long as my heart
got rhythm

!scream!
!exist!
go Jesus in the temple on 'em

let them hear our battle cry
let's crash this
private lynching
let loose our noosed neck
leave the gawking crowd
astounded
when Black girls

rise from the dust
they make of us

ALERT
Dashaan
I'm crying your name
Relisha
Alert
Taylor
I'm looking for you
Dayana
even if no one else is
Talisha
call back
Morgan
come back
Jacqueline
Robin
Aniya
ALERT *OLUWATOYIN*
ALERT *OLUWATOYIN*
ALERT *OLUWATOYIN*
ALERT
ALERT
ALERT

———————————

yeah, i flipped a table once
fucked they whole shit up

and i'd do it again
if that's what it takes for y'all
to see us

There has been no justice. There will be no peace!

He seemed so nice

he has two parents and a football trophy.
he holds the cigarette butt until he can put it in the garbage.
he takes out the trash and recycling and wheels the cans back
    into the yard.
he curbs the dog.
he waves at you while mowing the lawn.
irons his confederate flag before he lays it across the hood of
    his pickup.
he signals before turns.
taught to hunt like his daddy.
        a man who takes his life out on everyone else.
cleans his gun before he shoots.
picks up the cans & shells after practice.
scopes game & attacks when least expected.
manipulates the art of silence.

& blinking, finally, dabs the sweat off his brow,
stands over this bloodied once in a blue
bo(d)y.

'cause nice men always take out the trash, don't they?

what's the most beautiful thing?

what's the most beautiful thing?
    speak its name aloud

imagine,
every time you get a
good thing—
one of the most beautiful things must die!

imagine, that
good thing you get is justice.
how many beautiful things will die for that?

for (insert name)

you never realize how to label a dream
until you want to tell your children apart
you never realize you'll forget how to tell your children apart
    when you have a stomach full of shrapnel from the death
    of some other mother's son

don't want your baby to........
die on a cross like (insert name)
or in a crosswalk like (insert name)

you don't want him to be like (insert name) lying in middle of
    the street

not another (insert name) crying he can't breathe

or (insert name) shot on that doorstep
'cause Black fist against door
equates fist against body
'cause guns ring out
more than doorbells

or (insert name)'s brains
splattered
in that alley—'cause a cell phone could be a lot of things in the
    dark
but an unregistered 9mm semiautomatic fired over the
    shoulder
can only be one thing
—an eraser

a broken taillight in broad daylight
—a reaper

eye contact. a counterfeit bill.
—a death wish

you ain't gon' let your son go out like
how they let (insert name) run

just far enough to think
himself safe
before they shot

you won't let the last time you see him
                whole
be like when
they threw (insert name) in the back of that van

hands cuffed behind his back like (insert name) but he still
    managed to shoot himself like (insert name)

his spine in pieces like (insert name)

you want him to be home
like when they put curfew on (insert name)'s soul—too Black
    to be out at night

you ain't gonna be asking the news
why they say (insert name) when they really mean (insert
    name)
got Obama & Kamala callin' us (insert name)
like they don't sit around callin' them (insert name)

'cause isn't that the right word?
'cause you know ALL lives matter
—except (insert name)

how lucky am i,
to have (insert name)
in my bloodline
holy—the way (insert name) keeps pushing my pen from
    heaven

i flap my gums
show the world the fist in my throat
in honor of (insert name)

but my mother begs me home from the protest
says she can't go through what she went through with (insert
    name)
says
this hype over (insert name)
will die just like
(insert name)

and i tell her
i'd rather die for (insert name)
—a million times—
than die like (insert name)
—once

My mind is a gun

My thoughts the bullets
My mouth got a trigger, bitch don't make me pull it
Right at the backa yo head like mullets, spill ya IQ
Have you thinking that if they read the Bible
transgressions committed, can't be held liable
But they be trifling, sinning way more than I do
Catholic school my whole life, I was lied to
Reconcile with fists if they tried you
Raised to sing hosanna in the highest
But I don't see Zion
If I admit Rihanna's the finest
I'd be lyin' if I ain't say shit had me cryin
'til I realized Jah nuh play 'bout this conquering lion

I ain't know you could kill yourself 'til I was 15
got the call my homie wouldn't see 16
Thought that devil would miss me
Couple years later death came to kiss me
The fuckery—made me think I don't deserve luxury
I stayed for every soul that look up to me
stopped tryna make life look buttery
that's just a summary

Never bought a gun 'cause
I kept watching my niggas die

couldn't believe my eyes
when I contemplated suicide
Barrel to my medulla
it was me on two sides
Fools' pride
I think back on it while I'm poolside
smooth thighs, elevated as reparations
for those who died for me to lay here celebratin'
every occasion that led to my coronation

Unethical
mans Died for Amerikkka
wasn't no miracle
alla they mama's hysterical
it's clerical
the way I cleaned up my act is a parable
comparable to that son prodigal
but I'm a daughter
so I breathe life into the world with broken waters
resurrecting redemption after the slaughter
every line originally thought of

No I never started from the bottom
Had my mama
she the reason I hafta go harder
I'm smarter
than every enemy that tried to barter
a poisonous apple to trick me inna being a martyr

I survived every attempt at my demise
took way too long to realize I am the prize
just raised my price
don't really matter if you ask nice
I get aggressive if I gotta tell yo ass twice

And I mean that disrespectfully
don't check for me
unless your financier dun cut that check for me

all of the women in me are Black

i know this because i hear them chompin' and chattin' always tal'm 'bout what they not gon' do after ship and sail and death and work and birth and ever since i found out money was made out of cotton i wished there was such a thing as a bushel of trash fast food 'cause the lil Black girls in me always wanted to plant some mickey seeds to grow some mickey trees with mickey leaves to weave up some McDonald's money until the women in me were like nah sis we wasn't in them fields sunup to sundown for no computerized chicken we got food seasoned with 400 years of struggle and some Lawry's at home and i guess there are some horrors no time nor tide can wash away and if anyone would know it would be these Black ass women in me who got micro braids that turn cornrow in a moment's glance and will mollywhop and snatch your wig back way back to your wig cap and don't care who dun it these women gon' whoop all y'all asses and call you in for supper with your eye blacked 'cause the women in me know how to heal this with that and that with this will put the ice in your lemonade and on your forehead after a motherly kiss my ass for stepping out of bounds in the first place 'cause they saw it coming yes imagine one woman's intuition and then consider the telepathy of all the women in me who been wronged by men they know didn't know how to sacrifice for anyone let alone themselves and preyed on the woman that the women in me would become yet the women in me never fled just fought 'cause what more is freedom to a group of Black women than a kickback wine down flappin' lip 'bout whatchamacallit & them badass kids with her sistas at the heart of a woman they worked so hard to keep standing less over a stove moreover a legacy much like the Black women in the Black woman before me to set a blueprint for the Black women in the Black woman beyond me and ain't no better respite for the Black women in me than a stone cold stare and a wait 'til we get home knowing they actually have one.

i must tell you

Freddie Gray and i
share the same birthday

i must tell you
this is not the first time
a Black man dies
after locking eyes

i must tell you
how blessed we are
to be hashtagged
while breathing

i must tell you
a murderer's breath is
the homicide note
no one ever writes

i must tell you
this is the uncreation story
of a Black man
in a Christ-stained body

i must tell you
Freddie was genesis
& on the 7th day he rested

i must tell you
when the city is on fire
the summer comes early

i must tell you
i smile
in amazement
at fury-lit streets

i must tell you
this poem
is a famished reflection

i must tell you
this poem
has a bellyful
of Black flesh
and bone

i must tell you
this poem
will eat YOU alive

i must tell you
this poem
licks the plate
when it's done

i must tell you
this poem
is never done

i must tell you
i pray
for the day it will end

i must tell you
when i pray
i keep one eye cracked
&
just a bit of space between my palms
hoping
a bit of God will seep through.

Dear Black Child

They are afraid of you.
They hear gunshots in your breath.
You got 44 caliber pigment.
More ammunition in your melanin
Than they have on their waistband.

The Blackest part of you is a closed mouth.

So cock your head
Let your mouth be barrel
Unsilenced
Speak bullet
Speak bloodshed

Dear Black child,
You don't fit the description.
We don't want to learn your name this way.

Tell them who you are
before your memory is gunsmoke.

Spitfire, too

In order to rise from its own ashes, a phoenix first must burn.

—OCTAVIA BUTLER

i carry the wood
       of men
i have never loved
       {in my mouth}
a strange man calls me *bitch*
a cop calls me *bitch*
my father calls me *bitch*
my abuser calls me   *bitch*
my girlfriend calls me *bitch*
when i remind her of her ex-boyfriend
& all of these men
lodge their wood
in my jaw
one way or another.
each bitch be a full cord
       —a season's worth of kindling.

the problem,
i do not sweat.
i spark!

my whole heart—a wick
each beat—a strike
while each tooth a lit match
my tongue
doused in butane
cautious not to swallow
        this is no metaphor
this is a recipe
        for fire.
i gnash
& out spews
the poem
        thee inferno
i speak
a 5 alarm
the stage
a brushfire.
the crowd
ablaze.
i ignite the venue!

& these men
& their wood
—ain't nothing more than a field of ashes
& this mouth
a charcoaled pit
microphone
or extinguisher

all i know is it
keeps me from
torching myself
this wood
once a burden
becomes the reason
i spit fire
a woman
completed by flames
& searing syllables
scorching my way to survival
even when fire silences women
like sun does skin when you bask in it
so quiet you ain't know you was charring
i start to think of Black as burning
        with radiance

or

        with churches
i am not opposed to burning things to the ground.
i have learned it is the only way to send a concrete message
    to god
i don't know what rises more,
souls of Black bodies
or smoke
& no one who's communed
with god
comes back to fill us in.

you've seen the news,
only the survivors are the storytellers.

each man's *bitch*
is a combustible woman's reason
to exhale
& his wood,
his downfall.
crumbling, he
asks me to be more water.
still wishing me
wet his wood.

heaven is an ocean i've yet to learn to swim
but i sure as hell know i can burn

The N Word

She called me a nigga . . .
and i stare at this girl
a couple slave masters
lighter than me,
scanning my face,
like my eyes gon' tell her
if it's okay or not.
i think of all the places folk go
to hear nigga,
say nigga . . .
the club.
the police academy.
the hbcu.
the poetry slam.
shout at me
and say stay on the mic.
shout at me
and say get free.
and aint that just like white folk?
to get you stuck—
and be privileged enough
to watch you fight your way out.
they welded nigga
in our heads;
expect to just take it

out our mouths.
made Jesus nigga on that cross
and in that red light crosswalk
where them niggas Big & Pac
died for our sins
made niggas wear chains
—ain't nigga a chain itself
—ain't nigga a mentality
—ain't she ever seen
a white nigga
call it redneck,
trailer trash
meth head

massa got as many names
as the devil do;
still mean nigga.
when this biracial one
fix they mouth to say nigga
but all you see is teeth
you know what half it's coming from . . .
guess she ain't seen the video
where the alternate me say
and who in thee fuck are you calling a nigga?
and she fix her mouth to say, "you"
'cause her bloodline used to watching a nigga hang
but she ain't know what'll make a nigga swing

Hypothesis:
a. see how fast one become nigga
when called nigga
b. See how fast 3/5 of a person
whoop yo whole ass

like i won't Shaq-attack
knock the nails out yo motherfucking backboard
leave yo head broken rim hanging
like every tooth you lose
is another nigga out of Rikers
and every drop of blood
is an ancestor getting their wings
instead,
i think of every nigga
they called my brother—
bleeding to death
me watching.
me knowing he wasn't.
i gave up metaphor
the day i watched a real thing
become a once was.
decided everything i say aloud
would be something i could keep,
something that is mine.

me saying nigga is not getting me killed
you saying nigga is killing the both of us

& i laugh
'cause i've learned
over
& again
it is the only thing
that retracts the trigger,
separates
my hands and yo neck
yo body and the morgue
my body and the cell.
peel back centuries
of you ain't welcome here,
decolonize this tongue,
whisper to myself,
this is mine, this is mine, this is mine
damn near in prayer.

& white people will only be able to refer to this as,
that one poem, where you know she says . . .
ooo, I shouldn't say it.

Ode to Fetty Wap written after Strip Club

A reading from the book of Willie Maxwell
chapter 679
verse 1738
And then Rap Gawd formed a man from the dust of the
auto-tune and breathed into his nostrils the breath of Remy
Martin, and the man became Fetty Wap.

Rap Gawd saw fit to make Fetty a counterpart. So He caused
the man to fall into a deep sleep; and while he was sleeping,
he took one of the man's eyes and then closed up the place
with flesh. Then the Rap Gawd made a woman from the eye
he had taken out of the man.

The creation story of Fetty,
the first trap rapper to make a hit song I might play at my
wedding

there's a choir of church mothers smiling down on the brown
boy that sings of a woman's worth in a culture destined to
nullify it

Do you know how long sisters been waiting for a brother to
willingly let us hit the bando?
especially after patiently explaining what the fuck that
means

(l'union fait la force)
Your music emblematic of the motto of Haiti
"unity makes strength"

We scream *SQUADDDD*
the weight of that base
hits hard
like Gawd's tears landing on glow in the dark floors
'cause Gawd does not just "cry"
He makes it rain
on a crowd of women in heels higher than most GPAs
dancing their way through nursing school
& out of some deadbeat's roach-filled one bedroom
& the fellas,
big brother arm wrapped shoulders
singing off-key about Ki's and pies and other shit they have
no real idea about
the only song in the club that allows a hetero male to gaze
into the eyes of another [suspected] hetero male and sing his
fucking heart out
make him feel more mathematician than murderer
spewing lyrics repping the urban district's finest cognac
this
is a Black man's
Sweet Caroline
oh, oh, oh!

Fetty, you got me
I, too, see heaven peering through the pearly gates smile of
that gap-toothed princess in your video

I, too, have a glock in my rari—in the form of a master's degree
but don't get it twisted this summa cum laude blaow anytime
a motherfucker think they know me!

& my trap may look a lot like a dimly lit café with semi-cold
Red Stripes and a microphone and a couple judges but I'll be
damned if anyone tell me I ain't a queen of this shit
& then I blink
& the bass subsides
& the song fades into another brother caring more about his
golden grill
than making the best of a family business

& she picks up her pride,
her purse
slides off the pole
disappears into a mixture of low-budget smoke machines
& catcalling men
with their wedding bands tangled in the drawstring of their
sweats

& another Saturday twerks itself into the crisp breeze of
Sunday morning

& the church mothers glance over the room covered in
government-issued confetti
& Gawd smiles
as they bellow in unison,
I want you to be mine again

gay grl

Boy: You gay or you grl?

gay grl gay
as fuck
don't wanna have to tell nobody she gay
or she grl
just wanna be gay & grl

gay grl on fire
got yo grl in my DMs
will take yo grl
love yo grl
marry yo grl
got yo grl unleashing her inner gay grl
got yo homophobic mama calling me daughter
got folk
coming home
and coming out
wooo, gay grl powerful!

gay grl outstretch arms
been crucified
been nailed
to bed

to dresser
to backseat

gay grl scared she gon' die
like blk boy
for being blk
looking blk
looking like blk boy
killed by blk gun
killed by blk boy
for being gay grl in
blk boy clothing

gay grl still dressed
still writin'
still spittin'
still fightin'
gay grl still breathin'
gay grl still grl,
boy,
don't you get it?
gay-grl-good
Gay, grl good

Dyke Privilege

is a homophobe's sworn enemy.
a uterus, trapped in a block of cement
trying to escape the wrath of the male gaze.
Dyke privilege is repetition.
is No, sir.
No. Sir.
I'm, no sir.

Dyke privilege is no, I don't wish to be a man.
is yes, I have been with a man.
is a memory of the men who laid me flat like a baby
back when I was a baby.

Dyke privilege is watching white gays swallow
        whole the Black femme
while you just butch
            enough to burn alive.

Dyke privilege gives new meaning to strong Black woman.
Meaning I don't fit.
Meaning rescue myself in silence or die trying.
Dyke privilege is being born
        fit for a casket.
my body the first burial.

my name a tombstone.
my legacy an abomination.

Dyke privilege is a game
of cat and mouth
Unworthy until a man deems me fuckable.
what good is a pussy he can't pipe,
too clogged with another woman's fingers and tongue
and time is all it takes for him to scissor his way into our
    bedroom.
ready to cum without an invite.
another reason
to stray far from the men's department.
to stand clear of closing doors.
to lock them behind me.

Dyke privilege is for girls like us
us ones
the Black ones
that don't get hashtags
don't get no tender love
no praise as god of the whole damned world
they're praying for you not to be you no more
even if not being you means you are no more.
the harder the girl
the ~~softer~~ shorter the life

Dyke privilege is bobos and frilly socks, just for me
dresses to sweet 16s for our mothers to see—
our pretty
one last time
before we graduate
to hoodies and shape-ups
and death threats

Dyke privilege don't erase the gender
better to erase the people
extinguish the flame
that burns through a drowning

Dyke privilege will drop flowers on an already blooming
    memory
hanging prayers in black gowns
Dyke privilege gon' bury us in the suit
we wished we wore for prom
lower our fancied corpse into the dirt they say we are
us girls
pillaged and plundered
but the news says our sexuality has nothing to do with it

Dyke privilege gets left for dead.
goes uncalculated.
Unreported.
Our love story debunked.

Our mutilated bodies labeled as friends or roommates
So even our skeletons
must come out the closet.

An Ode to *The Color Purple* or Black Women Bleed, too

Dear God,
I could write the most beautiful poem
but a dick to the throat
gets your attention.
a bullet to the head
gets her a rally
        in a vacant lot
I wonder . . .
how they say her body was
riddled
with bullets
wasn't nothin' funny.
wasn't no mystery.
only Black & blood

Who you think you is? You can't curse nobody. Look at you.
    You're Black, you're
poor, you're ugly, you're a woman, you're nothing at all!

sister! you have the right to be made silent
anything you say can and will be erased
and the killer goes free
I just stand back, see what the ground gon' look like.
See what kinda bodies they

put on there now . . .
Tanisha
Tarika
Rekia
Kendra
Darnisha
Aiyana
Sandra, sat in that jail,
*I sat in that jail 'til I near about done rot to death. I know what
it like*
*to wanna go somewhere and cain't. I know what it like to
wanna sing . . . and have*
it beat outta ya.
& the killer still goes free

I think it pisses cops off
when they walk by the color purple in a field
and can't shoot at it.
Don't nobody wanna say her name
Only want her to scream theirs
Scream daddy
Scream, Daddy don't
Scream don't
Please, don't hurt my kids.
Daddy, sinners have souls too.
him, too
dun forgot just how much woman
he actually is

dun forgot he been built in this body
just wanna lay wood and pipe
dun forgot this body be steeple
and forest
threatened by wind, fire
bullet and fist
the color purple
awarded to those
wounded in action
All my life I had to fight . . .
To be Black, woman,
Queer and breathing
all at once
is a war on its own.
but dear God,
i'm here.
and 'til you do right by me
i am learning
loving myself
is a deliberate act
like Black
seeing Black
for the first time
see it ain't the darkness
they say it is
& every moment in this Black
is a razor to the throat, but no slit
a resurrection

a homecoming
which is to say
everything
you done to me,
is coming RIGHT back!

My country 'tis of thee

Sweet land of liberty
Of thee I sing
Land where my kin has died
Shot down in broad dayliGht
Left them bleeding

My kin has gone to be
Somewhere more Heavenly
They're with the King
I know He shines his light
My angel since that night
They took your love from me
I'll keep fighting

Hypersensitivity

is a term made up by the devil to keep angels falling from grace
is shock treatment
is silver tape on the mouth, hands, feet
is a gag order
is an order of protection placed by yourself against yourself
is a sleep aid
induces a coma
is an antidepressant—keeps you asleep inside yourself
is a straitjacket—keeps you wild inside yourself,
won't let the inside out, only the outside in!
makes you uncomfortable
makes you a feeling
makes you a loner
makes you a color
that no one wants
does not make you a human
is white America
is Black America
is Latin America
is having all of these Americas in one America and not once
    feeling whole or home
is a body in the street from 3 pm to 9:47 pm
is a body bleeding and cuffed and dying
is a pointer/a trigger/a trigger finger/the chamber/the barrel/
    the bullet

is the last breath
is a response to stimulus that plucks a nerve in the accuser
    and has
nothing to do with the accused
is the time I tell a man he is not my daddy
and he calls me a bitch
is that statement coming from my daddy
is me missing my daddy
is me falling from grace
is me never being graceful
never being an angel
never being the devil
just being hyper
and sensitive

The New Black

Gay is . . .
Black face is . . .
Stop and frisk is . . .
Dead is . . .
the new Black
is currently so popular
that it rivals the traditional status
of Black as the most
reliably fashionable color

The new Black is *a room without a roof*
The new Black says you get to pick what side you're on
Cries to Oprah about
how it's our mentality
and not our skin color
that gets us gunned down
Then performs hands up don't shoot
at the Grammys
dressed like a limited edition Mickey Mouse

The new Black is the token on Disney and Nick
with no home and no family,
just a cellphone and a savior complex
that always answers their white friend's beckoning.
The new Black doesn't do hyphens or labels or Cosby

The new Black doesn't wanna be African-American, just
    American
The new Black has an Afro with a magnetic field that forces
    all of the iron in white people's blood to rush to their
    fingertips, attracting them directly to the scalp before
    permission is granted.
The new Black got a scholarship to the accredited college
    that's longing to become a university,
but needs to up diversity levels
The new Black plays cards against humanity
because putting sexist, racist bigotry in a box is the same as
    watching television
the new Black don't watch TV
But has subscriptions to every streaming platform
The new Black loves Wanda, Mama Payne, Grandma-ma, but
    fucking hates that purse-carrying, pistol-toting Madea.
The new Black is still waiting for Obama to change the world!
The new Black thinks Kanye will apologize.
The new Black forgets we have been afraid to speak up since
    cat-tailed skin
and cotton bristle pricked fingertips.
The new Black is a capsized slave ship swaddled in skin and
    bone

In the 1920s,
the Harlem Renaissance
was also known as
the "new negro movement"

As if the old negros
were any less chained.
Like there's a runaway R
scorched into the spine
of everyone claiming
"the new Black"
Like we ain't been
solar and soil powered
Like from the moon
the sky ain't Black
both night and day
Like Michael Jackson ain't moonwalk
his Black ass to heaven
Like his Black ain't absorb the light of the world
Like Black ain't the absorption of all that is light
And all these things will fade into darkness
and darkness will be the new Black
and Black will be the new . . .

Kathy Griffin is photographed holding bloodied head of Trump: THE HAND SPEAKS

Awww shit,
palm,
fingers,
thumb,
check!

Manipulation—
most literal translation
Latin root *manipulus*—
handful
of distraction
of propaganda

This country in the
tiny hands
of a man
not fit to carry it

I'm a hand full of knuckles
always knocking my way
into some mess
some photographer's gaze

it's not about how I
carry myself
it's all about what I
grip between my fingertips

I'm just a hand,
I can't be racist
she can
No one warrants racism
I could be the hand who deals it

My thumb,
could be the key
to live streaming
your murder on Facebook.
Don't you wanna go viral?

I could be the trunk
Twitter fingers branch out from
talk about horrible coverage
I invented *covfefe*
so you could laugh at memes
ignore Black lives
hate crimes
bombings

Could be the wax-covered hand
palm rolling

the locs of Lady Gaga,
Demi Lovato
Miley Cyrus
poorly positioning Rachel Dolezal's wigs
inserting celebrity injection needles
Taylor's hand
with Beyoncé's Grammy
Macklemore's hand
with Kendrick's Grammy
La La Land with *Moonlight*'s Oscar

a freedom writer
the prejudice Picasso
spray-painting nigger
giving Lebron's house a
splash of color

the white wannabe
writing the think piece
about how Black poets
romanticize white death
while skipping through
Kendrick's *Damn,*

I can't be that bad

just ask the handcuffed
wrists of

Shannon Richardson
mailing ricin-laced letters to
the White House
in order to frame her husband

I could be the hand that
just came to kill Black people

the pointer of a white jogger
fingering innocent Black teens
out of a lineup

the cashier
waving hello
at Emmett Till—
a death threat
soon come

any
officer/watchman/whiteman
with a trigger finger itching to kill

there's an image
in Black and white
the Black swinging
the white
smiling
and I think:

that's someone's father,
about his bound hands,
about the hands he will never hold again,
about the hand that tied the noose,
but that's old news

I'm not googling justice
for them

because Barron Trump is afraid
ain't that how this all starts,
a white person's fear?
probable cause
to warrant
a show of hands

Kathy,
you've learned white women
ain't safe outside the shadow
of a man.
see what it's like to be hung
out to dry

what about the hand that lynched Obama
or the hand that lynched Obama
or the hand that lynched two Obamas
branded & lit them on fire

what about the trembling
fists
when Michelle saw it
when Malia saw it
when Sasha saw it
when my 6-year-old niece saw it?

We are always expected
to let go.

This time I'm latching on for dear life
I did not commit the killing
I just brandished the trophy
the death of Donald
does not deliver us from evil

this image is ahead of its time
this time it's a head
covered in the blood
of centuries of injustice
after another presidency
from hell.

The beheading of Goliath
is a symbol of hope.
You have to attack the beast
where it hurts,
hoist the head up before

the crowd,
hear them rejoice
as they
dance in the crimson rain
dripping from its eyes
or its *whatever*

people want to see our pain

on paper
on stage
on skin
want to see us depressed
lie and say they wanna see us better
we think we get better
they say they love us
we say we love us
they say we think too highly of ourselves
say we don't listen to nobody
say they can't tell us nothing
when they told us love ourselves
and we did
and we do
and it's better than they could
so we wrong?
for getting better
for being better
start thinking maybe we took this self-love thing too far
start smilin' less
start cryin' more
start lovin' us like lovin' us needs a balance
like we need a balance
they said we wasn't enough happy
they say we not enough shattered

they see we too much—
potential
progression
profession
we start tellin' our story
show them our bruises
they toastin' in our name with the next motherfucker
say we think we Maya Angelous
why?
'cause *we stand alone and go forth as thousand?*
like victim and victor are that far-off
like pain don't make power
and they want to see our pain
right?

these days
we see Black
where we're not supposed to
less on the ground
more on a world stage
more on the 30 yard line
taking knees
taking Grammys
see Black magic
ain't what *they* say it was
we quickly learn
to stay away from *they*
we see white

and don't blend in
and don't help it stand out
'cause privilege
they can surely help themselves
'cause a cop car burns
and they alive enough to get mad about
but a brown body falls
and it just dead enough to be forgotten
when they see PRO BLACK
as anti police
don't see this ain't for them
or 'bout them
this fubu
and honestly being Black & woke
is extracurricular activity
so we write poems they'll only teach as electives
so we infiltrate schools & businesses
so we teach our own shit
serving all this good ratchet ghetto urban educated master's
    level
Assume the position
Back hunched
Pen gripped
Hand in motion
mouth to mic
or not
'cause fuck amplification
and phallic symbols

we be loud enough
Black enough
because us sisters
needed a fuck the police
of our own
and nobody wanna say her name
and *Friends* is still on repeat
and not *Roots*
and not *Living Single*
shit, not even *Girlfriends*
'cause too many people worried 'bout who we fucking and/or
    not fucking
and we still slaying
we still writing
we still winning
we still Black
still Black
still Black
and we here
that's a triumph all on its own.

Blk Rage

It is the night after the
election and I don't
smile.
I lie
awake. Wondering
what kind of ancestor
I will be.

I, the child of a hard
father that only
wanted soft
daughters,
learned to make a
perfect fist on my
own. Learned to
swing by watching,
by feeling.
I bark, like the dogs
do, loud and in the
face of danger.
Gnash my teeth &
secure all things vital.
I learned to fight
before I learned to
speak.

My hands grew into
grenades.
I learned I hold the
pin,
tight.
Learned, to explode
only when necessary.
Learned, 'tho I'm
always at war not
every room is a
battlefield.

I shout: *Black Joy*
across the world and
folks with smiles the
smell of green bean
casserole praise me
for not being
angry.

I been angry.
My fists paint holes
into walls.
I was 14 the first time
I stomped a man's
face into mashed
potatoes.
I used to pray

to a god who would
not come home.
A Black butch with a
slick tongue
and a hunger for
freedom
I'm the kind of sorry
no one teaches us to
forgive.

I Say: Blk Joy
They Hear: shuck &
jive
Think me palatable
(good Black).

Nah, this ain't what
enlightenment looks
like. I got a backpack
full of screwups and
screw yous.

There came a point
where tears were no
longer able to cleanse.
There are still days I
want out, but I'm no
better if I only save

myself. And right
now, there are people
lining the floors of
arenas to hear me tell
them
losing is at capacity.
Guess we going
to win.

Someone gave me a
pen
I wrote a spine into a
sack of skin.
Imagine me not angry
explaining to white
folks anti-racist work
ain't hashtagging or
posting a black box
not fit to hold my last
breath.
Or raising me up by
your white guilt
straps.
Anti-racism means
you're willing to die
for my kind of Black.
That built the country,
you wrote me out of.

What good is writing
poems to my unborn
when I got nieces and
nephews?

They shutting down 1
prison to build four
and got a bunk with
our last name on it.
They waiting for us to
forget we were
chosen
While I'm god's
daughter
my godson's father is
locked in a cage.

I don't write
metaphors about
caskets and burials.
Just another way for
the world to hold us
hostage.

Tell the dead I am
still here
Tell the here I am still
fighting

I live and learned to
walk on the seas
beneath and between
us.
The ship is sinking,
but I'm teaching us to
swim.
To wade in the
war zone.

Where our joy
endangers us.
Buying groceries.
Playing video games.
Enjoying ice cream.
In bed.
In a backyard.
In a parking lot.
On a wine train.

The men in my family
are still breathing and
that is a crime.
The women in my
family are
reproducing and that
is a crime.

I say: *We gon' make it*
Someday we'll all be
free
Be real Black for me
Alright
& I'm talking to god
on repeat

I was born Black,
woman & American
Bitterness beckons,
inspired by my mere
existence
Born waiting for *the*
land of the free to
bust a capitalist in my
head.

You think me being
angry is the problem?

I Say: *Black Joy*
And I mean, I forgive
my father.
I mean, F the police.
I mean, dismantle
white supremacy.
I mean I was zip-tied

one night,
Kettled on the
Manhattan Bridge the
next,
and lived to teach
your kids in the
morning.

I am everything
america threatens
to break
and the threat
and the break
and america itself.

What I'm saying is,
Nah, I'm not angry.
I'm coming.

I say: Black Joy and I
mean,
who are you
when I start taking
what I am owed?

Blk Joy

We gon' be ALRIGHT!

—KENDRICK LAMAR

My name is Roya Marsh and I am a Black poet who will not remain silent while this nation continues to murder Black people. I have a right to be angry. I have a right to be joyful. #BlackPoetsSpeakOut

Black Joy
Is real
Is native
Is not white
was here before y'all
Before God said let there be light
so y'all could witness a glimpse of what you been missing

Black
- is not a color; it absorbs all the colors of the visible spectrum and reflects none

Joy
- is a feeling of great pleasure or happiness

Black Joy looks like me
like him, her, them
It knows no gender
just knows
prosperity
in spite of white supremacy

Black Joy is solid
a stone
worthy of digging
excavating
a coveted jewel
to be held up to light
to sparkle and dazzle

Black Joy knows this poem is necessary
no matter what your judgments say
'cause you can't tell me Black Joy
won't break any scale you put it on
shit; can't tell me Black Joy ain't the scale
itself

Black Joy is contagious
so contagious folks got
caught appropriating

caught pinning Black against Black
Joy against Joy

Remy against Nicki
Kim against Nicki
Cardi against Nicki
Latto against Nicki
Rih against Bey
'cause healthy, wealthy Black femmes
just got too close to God

They only want to see us Black & Joyous
if they made us that way
but they cannot create Black Joy
the same way they created race
They cannot dictate our Blackness
They cannot dictate our happiness

Yeah it's true, once you go Black Joy
you never go back
ask the Kardashians
those black holes

Make a staple of Black Joy
Remember Black and happy can be synonymous
Whenever you hear the word Black
instead hear happy

Case in point:
In 2016, we bid farewell to the nation's first Happy President
February is Happy History month

Hollywood still won't cast Happy people to play our Happy
    ourselves
Yet another Happy body is found slain

all the more reason to preserve this
shield
this force field of fortune
no hot commodity
to be bought
bootlegged
Kylie lipkit
backshot
brainwash
Be your happiest when your mouth is open
Be your Blackest when your mouth is open

Shout it!
Shout Black!
Shout Joy!

Remember, white supremacy is a beast that feeds on
    attention

Be happier. Be hungrier. Starve it. Leave it nothing but the
    bones!

these soiled hands

have held more dead
than diplomas.
hold my own dead
inside my body
outside my body
hold my diplomas
drop some knowledge
hold my pen
let truth loose
take the long route
look at myself
my reflection
is an ocean of triumph
swim in it
survive

Notes

"What are the rights to your existence?": This poem references the Miranda warning.

"Scorpion Unit: elegy for Tyre Nichols": The SCORPION unit, which stands for Street Crimes Operation to Restore Peace in Our Neighborhoods, was "permanently" deactivated by the Memphis Police Department, a day after officials released footage of the brutal police murder of Tyre Nichols. The SCORPION unit, which launched in November 2021, encompassed forty officers split into four teams who patrolled "high crime hotspots" (read: racial profiling) throughout Memphis. Ivan Pereira and Meredith Deliso, "What was the SCORPION unit, the now-deactivated police task force at the center of Tyre Nicols' death?" ABC News, January 28, 2023, https://abcnews.go.com/amp/US/scorpion-unit-memphis -police-task-force-center-tyre/story?id=96720313.

"Ode to Fetty Wap written after Strip Club": This poem references the music and lyrics of Fetty Wap.

"An Ode to *The Color Purple* or Black Women Bleed, too": This poem makes reference to Alice Walker's *The Color Purple* and the 1985 film directed by Steven Spielberg and written by Menno Meyjes.

"My country 'tis of thee": "America," popularly known as "My Country, 'Tis of Thee," was written by Samuel Francis Smith.

"Kathy Griffin is photographed holding bloodied head

of Trump: THE HAND SPEAKS": This is a persona poem referencing the image of the comedian Kathy Griffin holding a bloody mask of the forty-fifth president's head. The poem is told from the perspective of Griffin's hand, which points the finger and takes the blame. This photo had a grave impact on Griffin's career. Tara Suter, "Kathy Griffin didn't realize 'how serious' DOJ was about charging her over Trump head photo," *The Hill*, January 23, 2024, https://thehill.com/blogs/in-the-know/4425263-kathy-griffin-doj-trump-head-photo/.

Acknowledgments

To the Bronx be the Glory!

It is hard to acknowledge anything else when the world is on fire, but joy is the only thing that helps me extinguish the flames. I write with the knowledge that none of us are free until all of us are free.

I am grateful to all editors and publications that have put forth an iteration of pieces in this book.

"QTNA" was published in 2022 in *Poetry Super Highway*.

An earlier version of "Dyke Privilege" was published in 2022 by America Hates US.

"He seemed so nice" was published in 2020 by America Hates US.

"Ode to Fetty Wap written after Strip Club" was published in 2018 in *The BreakBeat Poets Vol. 2: Black Girl Magic* and *Poetry* magazine.

To my agent, Amanda, thank you for your constant support, encouragement, and allyship throughout this process! Thank you for teaching me and seeing me (even before I was ready to be seen). This process would not be the same without your stewardship.

To Jackson and Ben, my editors at MCD, I am grateful for your exceptional minds and eyes being lent to this manuscript.

Your intentional questions and thoughts helped to bring this book to completion.

To my family, given and chosen, I could not have written any of these poems without your love and the lessons we've learned together. Tamara and Z, thank you for being my family. Iloveyou!

To EbonyJanice and BGM Dakar, I am so honored to have journeyed home with you all.

I am grateful to all the educators, writers, and activists who cultivate healthy and supportive learning environments. Special thanks to Lambda Literary (and all my students!), the Adirondack Center for Writing, City Lore, the Bronx is Reading and our Bronx Poet Laureates, Bronx Bound Books, Heather Ostman and WCC, and the many other schools and organizations that allowed me to mentor their students and writers.

I am ever grateful for every student who has trusted me with their stories and their voices. This book and everything else I do is to remind you that there is no better time than the present to be your fullest and most liberated self.

Dear reader: I am grateful for you and your attention. Because of you, this book lives another day. If there was a piece in this collection that called you by name, listen. Take from it what you need. Live.

In the midst of it all, joy.